Mr. Lewis,

How are you? [T]he Silver Chair was [a b]ook, but I felt so ba[d] for Jill. I'm glad she and Eustace stood up to those bullies at their school in the end.

What was it like for you when you were in school?

All best wishes,

Francine

DEAR MR. LEWIS,

MY NAME IS SYDNEY, AND I AM NINE YEARS OLD. I JUST FINISHED THE LAST BATTLE, AND IT WAS GOOD, BUT SAD. I'VE REALLY LIKED ALL SEVEN OF THE NARNIA BOOKS SO FAR. ARE YOU WRITING THE NEXT ONE? I CAN'T WAIT TO READ IT!

SINCERELY,

SYDNEY

For my sons, Timothy and Lucas

Thank you to Douglas Gresham, the C. S. Lewis Company Ltd., and the Marion E. Wade Center for their assistance in researching and fact-checking this book. Any errors that remain are my own.

C. S. Lewis: Letters to Children. Copyright © CS Lewis Pte 1985.

Balzer + Bray is an imprint of HarperCollins Publishers.

Through the Wardrobe: How C. S. Lewis Created Narnia
Copyright © 2020 by Lina Maslo

Library of Congress Control Number: 2019935927
ISBN 978-0-06-279856-5

The artist used a dip pen, India inks, and acrylics on watercolor paper to create the illustrations for this book.
Typography by Dana Fritts
20 21 22 23 24 SCP 10 9 8 7 6 5 4 3 2 1
❖
First Edition

Through the Wardrobe

How C. S. Lewis Created Narnia

LINA MASLO

BALZER + BRAY
An Imprint of HarperCollinsPublishers

Clive Staples Lewis did not like his name.
He imagined himself as more of a . . . Jack.
When he was four years old, he changed it.
    As he grew, Jack didn't always like the world he lived in.
So he would imagine and write about other worlds.

The drizzly clouds of Ireland
kept Jack and his brother, Warnie,
inside much of the time.
But they didn't mind.

Their house had lonely, whispering rooms
that craved company.

Hallways that begged for wandering.

And books! Two-deep on shelves
and tumbling off tables.

The brothers claimed a space in the attic.
There, they read about talking animals and knights in armor,
gazed out at the harbor of ships leaving to explore faraway lands,

and wrote stories about a world called Boxen, where dressed-up frogs and mice and rabbits argued about politics and went on quests to defeat evil cats.

When the sky was clear, Jack and Warnie rode
their bicycles, and Jack would imagine that he
spotted animals from his favorite books:

Was that Peter Rabbit sneaking into a garden?
Or Squirrel Nutkin floating by on a raft?

Once, when Jack's cousins came to visit, they
climbed into a wardrobe that had been carved by their
grandfather and listened as Jack told exciting stories.

But when Jack was nine, his mother became sick and died.

And his wonder-filled world began to crumble.

Soon after, he was sent to boarding school in England, where he had a horrible experience.

Jack didn't fit in with the other boys,
and sometimes they were mean to him.

Jack couldn't understand . . .

Why did God create a world where people
were so cruel?

Where mothers of young boys died, and children
were sent far from home?

So he withdrew into his books—
into worlds of honor and friendship and love.
And he wrote stories of brave heroes.

Jack begged to be taken out of school.
A private tutor helped him finish his studies
and encouraged Jack to become a teacher.

But Jack was determined to be a writer.

Just as he entered college, though, a war began, and he enlisted in the army.

For months, Jack lived in muddy trenches filled with bullets and bombs.

To escape the horrors around him, he wrote poetry.

Then, during a battle, he was injured.

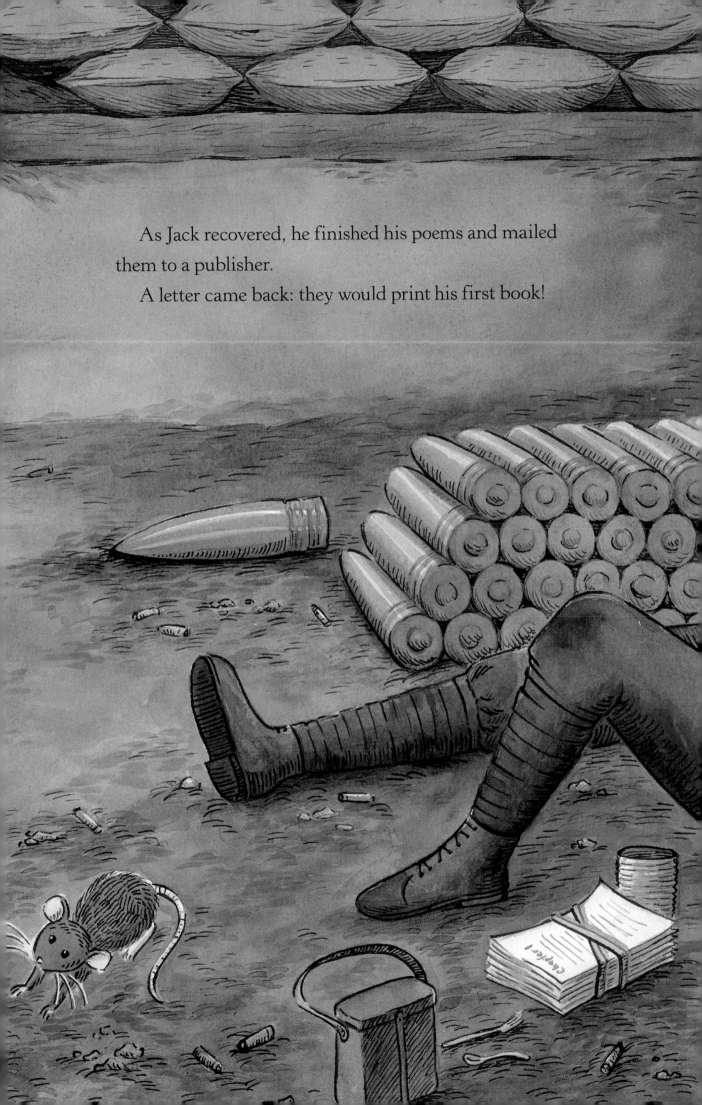

As Jack recovered, he finished his poems and mailed them to a publisher.

A letter came back: they would print his first book!

But even as his dreams of being a writer were coming true,
Jack's experiences in life and the war darkened his thoughts,
and he pushed his imagination away.

When the war ended, he returned to Oxford and
eventually became a teacher.

Years went by and slowly he began to believe again—
in hope and in happiness, in God,
in himself, and in his ability to tell stories—
and he went on to write book after book after book:
about pain and faith and love;
about medieval times;
about people discovering strange planets.

He became a well-known author.

But in the back of his mind, Jack had characters waiting for a story of their own, ones who didn't quite fit into the books he was writing for adults:

the chivalrous mice and talking animals of his boyhood;

a faun, shivering in snow;

a majestic lion;

and a fearfully beautiful queen on a sled.

What could he do with them?

Before he found his answer, a second world war began. Cities were being attacked, and children were sent to smaller towns like Oxford. Jack's injuries kept him from fighting, so he offered to take in evacuees.

One day, a little girl asked him if there was anything behind the old wardrobe—the one Jack and Warnie had had since they were boys.

What did she dream could be behind it?

Jack decided to write a fairy tale for her and other evacuees, about a land unlike the dreary one they lived in, and about the characters in his imagination.

He scribbled down the beginning and showed the people around him.

A few liked it, but some of Jack's friends, and even his publisher, didn't think it was a good idea.

One friend, an author named J. R. R. Tolkien, hated it!

Talking animals, mythical creatures, *and* Father Christmas in one book?

It didn't make sense.

Jack was so discouraged, he put aside the story.

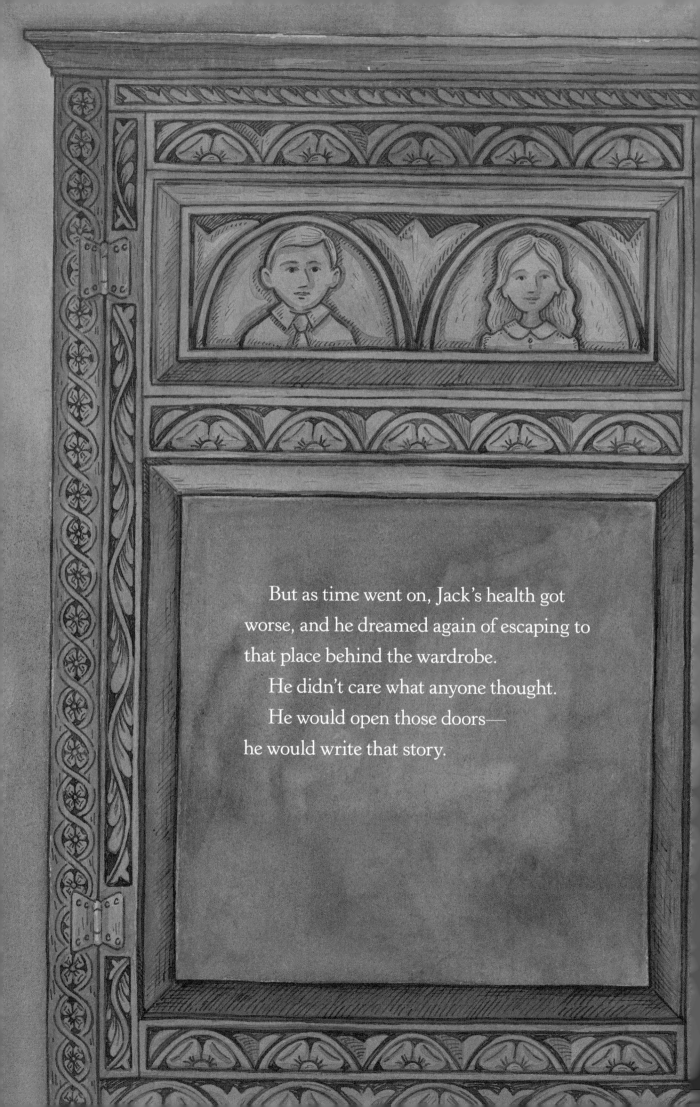

But as time went on, Jack's health got
worse, and he dreamed again of escaping to
that place behind the wardrobe.
He didn't care what anyone thought.
He would open those doors—
he would write that story.

It began with four children
who had been sent far from home
during the war.
　It was raining, and they were stuck
inside a house of endless hallways.
　They found a wardrobe
and crawled in.
　But as they pushed back the old fur coats,
they fell into a magical realm . . .

of talking animals and knights in armor,
of fauns and queens and a lion named Aslan,
of battles between good and evil,

where one learns things like courage and love and forgiveness.

A world called Narnia.

When the book *The Lion, the Witch and the Wardrobe* was released, children and grown-ups loved it!

They wrote letters to Jack asking for more stories.

So Jack brought them back to Narnia . . .

to awaken the trees and the waters,
and bring the badgers and squirrels
and hares out of hiding.

To sail through nightmares and darkness and dragony
thoughts, toward the sweet waters of Aslan's country.

In Narnia, you learned to stand up to bullies.

And that the worst moments of your life were only leading you to become the person you were meant to be.

Narnia began with a song
that created mountains and valleys

and a tree with apples
that could heal a dying mother
and answer the prayer of a boy.

Narnia ended with a terrible battle—
and with a door.

But the door that closed on Narnia
opened to a new land so breathtaking,
even Jack could barely describe it.

By the time the seventh Narnia book was published, Jack had become a famous children's book author.

He received numerous letters from his readers.

People asked how he knew what stories children liked.

He said he wrote what he would have liked to read as a child . . . *and* as an adult.

Some of the letters came from an American author named Joy.

Jack and Joy wrote to each other many times. Finally they met, and later fell in love.

They married, and Jack adopted Joy's sons, David and Douglas.

Though Joy only lived as Jack's wife for a few years, they were the happiest of his life.

And children continued to write
and ask for more stories about Narnia.
But this time, Jack was finished.
This time, it was up to others—
to discover a world only they could imagine
and to find the door they were destined to open.

Family

Clive Staples Lewis was born on November 29, 1898, in Belfast, Ireland, to Albert James Lewis and Florence ("Flora") Augusta Hamilton Lewis. His father was a lawyer. His mother received degrees in mathematics and logic. One of Jack's grandfathers owned a shipbuilding firm in Belfast and the other was a Church of Ireland clergyman.

Jack's mother took him and his brother, Warnie, on trips to the coast most summers, but she died of abdominal cancer when Jack was nine years old. His father had a difficult time coping with his wife's loss and became distant. Sometimes, the boys felt that they had lost both of their parents when their mother died. When Jack was thirty, his father also died of cancer.

Jack's older brother, Warren Lewis, was born three years earlier than Jack. Jack and Warnie were very close all their lives. Warnie made a career in the army, and after he retired, he wrote several books on French history.

When Jack was eighteen, he became friends with another student at Oxford, named Paddy Moore. Jack and Paddy swore to each other that they would care for the other's parent if either of them died. Paddy died in the war, so Jack took on the care of his mother, Janie Moore, and his sister, Maureen. Together, Mrs. Moore, Jack, and Warnie bought a house in Oxford they called the Kilns. They all spent the rest of their lives there.

Education

From a young age, Jack had a governess, and his mother taught him French and Latin. After his mother's death, Jack attended several boarding schools in England and Ireland: Wynyard School in Watford, Hertfordshire; Campbell College in Belfast very briefly; then Cherbourg House and Malvern College in Malvern. After Jack wrote many letters begging to get out of boarding school, his father sent him to the man who had once been his own teacher: W. T. Kirkpatrick, who lived in Great Bookham, Surrey. Under his tutelage, Jack thrived in his studies. He learned Greek, Latin, French, Italian, and German. He read poetry, such as Homer's *Iliad*, in its original language. He was, however, very bad at math no matter how hard he studied. Still, he was awarded a scholarship to attend University College at Oxford. There he received degrees in classical honor moderations (Greek and Latin literature), greats (philosophy and ancient history), and English.

After graduating, Jack was elected to teach English and philosophy at Magdalen College in Oxford. He would spend the next thirty years lecturing and tutoring there. After that, Jack was a professor of medieval and Renaissance English literature at Cambridge University until he retired.

The Wars

In August of 1914, England joined the First World War. Jack enlisted in June of 1917, and his first day in the trenches was on his nineteenth birthday. He was eventually wounded (by friendly fire), and by the time he recovered from his injuries, the war was over. Jack returned to Oxford, but many of his friends and fellow students did not.

Jack was forty when the Second World War began. Because of his wounds from the First World War, Jack didn't have to go and fight. Instead, he joined the Home Guard and helped patrol the streets at night. He also took in several groups of evacuee children during the war.

Faith

Jack was raised in an Irish Protestant family, but he didn't automatically accept the Christian faith. When his mother became sick, Jack prayed for her healing, but she died. Then, after witnessing and experiencing abuse at several boarding schools from both headmasters and students, he became angry at God for creating the world and gave up on his faith. During WWI, Jack saw pain and death, which further confirmed his belief in an unjust world.

But from childhood, Jack was also enthralled with a sensation he called "Joy." He searched for the source of his "Joy," and in his early thirties, he found it in Christianity. Jack later wrote about his journey of faith in his autobiography, *Surprised by Joy*, and the themes of faith and Christianity made their way into much of his writing, including the Chronicles of Narnia.

The Inklings

Jack and a small group of writers formed a critique group called the Inklings that met regularly for about twenty years. They gathered twice a week in a pub (usually the Eagle and Child) in Oxford or in Jack's rooms at Magdalen College to discuss and critique what they were reading and writing. One member of the Inklings was the author J. R. R. Tolkien. He and Jack became good friends, and together they decided that since there weren't enough books like the ones they liked to read, they would write some themselves. They sometimes disagreed but greatly influenced each other's work. Without Jack's encouragement, Tolkien said that he might have never finished the Lord of the Rings.

Writing Career

Jack's first book, *Spirits in Bondage*, was published when he was twenty years old. For over a decade after the war, Jack struggled with creativity, but in his thirties he went on to write many books.

Jack became famous in Britain and the United States after the success of *The Great Divorce* and *The Screwtape Letters*, and he was featured on the cover of *Time* magazine in 1947. He also hosted a series of talks about faith on BBC Radio during the Second World War, which were then published in the book *Mere Christianity*. The Chronicles of Narnia were published when Jack was in his fifties.

Love and Marriage

When Jack was in his early fifties, he received a letter from an American writer named Joy Davidman Gresham. Her letters were clever and funny. Some time later, Joy moved to England with her two sons but soon after realized she was not going to be able to stay—her visa was about to expire. Jack offered to marry her in a civil ceremony so she could live in England. It was not until later, when Joy was diagnosed with cancer and lying on her deathbed, that Jack realized he was in love with her, and they were married by a clergyman. Joy lived a few more years, and they had a happy marriage. He officially adopted her two sons, David and Douglas Gresham. After a few years, her cancer came back, and she died at the age of forty-five. Jack wrote *A Grief Observed* about the pain he felt over her loss and published it anonymously. He died a few years after Joy did.

. . . AND OTHER INTERESTING FACTS:

Jack had an Irish nurse named **Lizzie Endicott** who helped care for him when he was young. She told him Irish myths and folktales about leprechauns and fairies. One day, Jack and his brother, Warnie, found the end of the rainbow and dug for gold. They didn't find any, but their father fell in the hole on his way home.

When Jack was a boy, Warnie made a **toy garden** for him out of the lid of a cookie tin; moss, branches, flowers, and leaves were arranged to make a small landscape. It was one of Jack's most vivid memories as a child, a moment that opened his eyes to the beauty of nature and made him long for a different world.

Two boarding schools that Jack attended claim to have the gas **lamppost** that inspired the one that appears in Narnia: Malvern College and Campbell College.

Jack loved **mice**. He never set traps for them. He sometimes imagined talking to them late at night when he stayed up writing. During WWI, when shells were loudly dropping and exploding around him, a mouse huddled up next to him and stayed there until the noise ended.

When Jack's publisher was looking for an illustrator for the Chronicles of Narnia, J. R. R. Tolkien recommended **Pauline Baynes,** who had illustrated some of his own work. At first, Jack wasn't too happy with her illustrations. He thought Pauline couldn't draw children or lions well. But later he went on to thank Pauline for her work and contribution to the success of the books.

Jack saw the name **Narnia** on an atlas of ancient Italy. The town is now called Narni and is in the region of Umbria. Also, probably coincidentally, one saint from Narni, Italy, is the Blessed Lucy Brocadelli, also called **Blessed Lucy of Narni.**

The main character in *The Lion, the Witch and the Wardrobe*, Lucy Pevensie, is named after **Lucy Barfield,** Jack's goddaughter and the daughter of Owen Barfield, Jack's good friend and one of the members of the Inklings.

The character of Lucy is also based on a girl named **June Flewett** who stayed at the Kilns during WWII. She was sixteen years old, a devout Catholic, and an aspiring actress. One of her favorite authors was C. S. Lewis. For a while, she had no idea that Jack was C. S. Lewis and was shocked when she found out. June lived in the household for two years, and Jack called her "the most selfless person I have ever known."

Aslan means "lion" in Turkish.

The character **Puddleglum**, who first appears in *The Silver Chair*, is based on Jack's gardener, Fred Paxford, who said the gloomiest things but expected everything to turn out all right.

During WWII, many food items, among other things, were rationed. That meant people could only have a small amount of tea, sugar, eggs, and other items. Candy was rare, and one favorite for British children was **Turkish delight**. It's no surprise, then, that at that time, a child might sell out his siblings for an endless supply of sweets.

Jack died on the same day that American president **John F. Kennedy** was shot—Friday, November 22, 1963.

Some of Jack's **favorite children's books** were: Beatrix Potter's stories, especially *The Tale of Squirrel Nutkin; Gulliver's Travels* by Jonathan Swift; Edith Nesbit's *Five Children and It, The Phoenix and the Carpet, The Story of the Amulet,* and others; *The Wind in the Willows* by Kenneth Grahame; and George MacDonald's *The Princess and the Goblin.*

The **wardrobe** in this book was handmade by Jack's grandfather Richard Lewis. After his father's death, Jack moved the wardrobe from Ireland to his home in England. It now stands in the Marion E. Wade Center at Wheaton College in Illinois. In *The Lion, the Witch and the Wardrobe* the wardrobe that Lucy enters is described as "a perfectly ordinary wardrobe," the kind with "a looking-glass in its door." A wardrobe more closely resembling this description stood in Jack's bedroom at the Kilns and is now at Westmont College in Santa Barbara, California. Both wardrobes are available for viewing.

Chronicles of Narnia Order of Publication

The Lion, the Witch and the Wardrobe (1950)

Prince Caspian (1951)

The Voyage of the *Dawn Treader* (1952)

The Silver Chair (1953)

The Horse and His Boy (1954)

The Magician's Nephew (1955)

The Last Battle (1956)

BIBLIOGRAPHY

Cording, Ruth James. *C. S. Lewis: A Celebration of His Early Life*. Nashville: Broadman and Holman Publishers, 2000.

Dorsett, Lyle W., and Marjorie Lamp Mead, eds. *C. S. Lewis: Letters to Children*. New York: Simon and Schuster, 1985.

Duriez, Colin. *The C. S. Lewis Chronicles: The Indispensable Biography of the Creator of Narnia, Full of Little-Known Facts, Events, and Miscellany*. New York: BlueBridge, 2005.

Gilbert, Douglas, and Clyde S. Kilby. *C. S. Lewis: Images of His World*. Grand Rapids, MI: W. B. Eerdmans, 2005.

Green, Roger Lancelyn, and Walter Hooper. *C. S. Lewis: A Biography*. New York: Harcourt, 1974.

Gresham, Douglas. *Jack's Life*. Nashville: Broadman & Holman Publishers, 2005.

Hooper, Walter. *Through Joy and Beyond: A Pictorial Biography of C. S. Lewis*. New York: Macmillan, 1982.

Jacobs, Alan. *The Narnian*. San Francisco: HarperSanFrancisco, 2005.

McGrath, Alister. *C. S. Lewis: A Life*. Carol Stream, IL: Tyndale House Publishers, 2013.

Sayer, George. *Jack: A Life of C. S. Lewis*. Wheaton, IL: Crossway Books, 1988.

Sibley, Brian. *The Land of Narnia*. New York: Harper & Row Publishers, 1990.

Works by Jack (C. S. Lewis) consulted for this book:

Lewis, C. S. *Spirits in Bondage*. New York: HarperOne, 1919.

Lewis, C. S. *The Chronicles of Narnia*. New York: HarperCollins Publishers, 1950, 1951, 1952, 1953, 1954, 1955, 1956.

Lewis, C. S. *Surprised by Joy*. New York: HarperOne, 1955.

Lewis, C. S. *Of Other Worlds*. New York: Harcourt, Brace & World, Inc., 1966.

Lewis, C. S. and W. H. Lewis. *Boxen: Childhood Chronicles Before Narnia*. London: HarperCollins Publishers, 2008.

Dear Hila,

Thank you so much for your lovely letter and picture. Reepicheep has just the right, perky expression. I love real mice! There are lots in my rooms in College, but I have never set a trap. When I sit up late working they poke their heads out from behind the curtains just as if they were saying, "Hi! Time for you to go to bed. We want to come out and play."

All good wishes,
Lewis

Dear Francine,

I was at three schools (all boarding schools) of which two were very horrid. I never hated anything so much, not even the front line trenches in World War I. Indeed, the story is far too horrid to tell anyone of your age.

With all best wishes,
Yours sincerely,
C. S. Lewis

Dear Joan,

What really
1. Always try to
   to make quite
   make sure your se
   anything else.
2. Always prefer t
   the long, vague
3. Never use abs
   concrete ones
4. Don't use adject
   us how you want us
   thing you are descri
   of telling us a thin
   it so that we'll b
   say it was "delightf
   "delightful" when
   description. You see
   (horrifying, wonderfu
   to your readers "Plea
   my job f